MW01138652

The Mysterious Ancient MAYA

by L. L. Owens

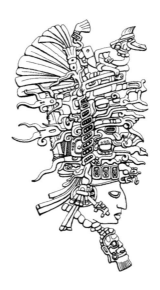

Perfection Learning®

About the Author

Lisa L. Owens grew up in the Midwest. She has been writing since she was a young girl, and she has always enjoyed learning about how people lived in ancient times.

She currently works as a writer and editor in Seattle, where she lives with her husband, Timothy Johnson.

Other books by Ms. Owens include *Tales of Greek Mythology, Tales of Greek Mythology II, Eye on Ancient Egypt, Looking Back at Ancient Greece,* and *Inside Ancient Rome.*

Image credits

Illustration: Margaret Sanfilippo: pp.19, 34, Michael Aspengren: pp. 48–49
Book Design: Randy K. Messer

© Danny Lehman/CORBIS cover; © Craig Lovell/CORBIS 20;
© Werner Forman/Art Resource, NY. pp. 39 (bottom), 46

Image Credits: ArtToday (some images copyright www.arttoday.com) pp. 1, 3, 9 (top), 10, 14, 16, 17, 18, 21, 24 (all), 26, 28, 30, 33, 36, 38, 39 (top); Corel pp. 6, 7, 9 (side image), 11, 12, 13, 15, 22, 25, 29, 31, 41; Randy Messer pp. 27, 45

For information, contact
Perfection Learning® Corporation,
1000 North Second Avenue,
P.O. Box 500, Logan, Iowa 51546-0500.
Tel: 1-800-831-4190 • Fax: 1-800-543-2745
perfectionlearning.com

PB ISBN-13: 978-0-7891-5732-2 ISBN-10: 0-7891-5732-4
RLB ISBN-13: 978-0-7569-0861-2 ISBN-10: 0-7569-0861-4

4 5 6 7 8 9 PP 13 12 11 10 09 08

Chac Mool, Chichén Itzá

Table of Contents

Mayan Empire

GULF OF
MEXICO

Chichén Itzá

YUCATÁN
PENINSULA

MAYA REGION

TABASCO

Mexico

CHIAPAS

Tikal

Belize

Guatemala

Quiriguá

Copan

Honduras

PACIFIC
OCEAN

El Salvador

Chapter

Setting the Scene

Ancient Mayan civilization is one of the greatest in history. It is also one of the most mysterious.

The Maya are a tribe of Central American Indians.

In ancient times, they lived in the Mexican areas of Yucatán, Chiapas, and Tabasco. They also lived in Guatemala, Honduras, and Belize.

They may have existed as early as 15,000 B.C. That's about 17,000 years—or 170 centuries—ago!

Ancient civilizations appeared as people formed cities and states. A civilization is people who live in a social group. Civilization includes a society's

- customs
- beliefs
- arts
- laws
- government
- **agriculture**
- **technology**

What Makes the Maya So Mysterious?

First, they lived so long ago. It's impossible to know exactly how they lived.

Second, their **culture** almost died out. That left few people to record their history.

And third, most of their writings were lost. The Spanish took over the Mayan area. They didn't care about Mayan history. So they destroyed much of what remained. This happened in the 16th century A.D.

Even so, modern **archaeologists** have learned a lot. They have studied Mayan **ruins**. They have discovered important **artifacts**. Their findings and **educated guesses** have helped put together pieces of the Mayan puzzle.

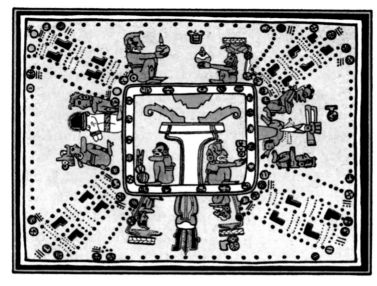

Mayan calendar

We do know a few things about the ancient Maya.

- They farmed the land.
- They built grand buildings.
- They studied the stars.
- They sailed the waters.
- They traded goods with neighbors.
- They invented their own calendar.
- They worshipped many gods.
- They created beautiful art.
- They used a mathematical system.
- They wrote in **hieroglyphics**.

Mayan history is often discussed in relation to important historical periods. Look at this timeline. It will help you understand how this great civilization changed over time.

Timeline of Mayan History

(All dates are best guesses.)

Paleo-Indian Period: 15,000–7000 B.C.

Probable origins of the Maya

Archaic Period: 7000–2000 B.C.

3114 B.C.   They start developing a calendar.

3000 B.C.   The Maya survive by hunting, gathering, and fishing.

Preclassic Period: 2000 B.C.–300 A.D.

2000 B.C.   They form villages in the lowlands. New social systems emerge.

250 A.D.   They form farming communities on the Yucatán **Peninsula.** They also build cities.

Mayan pyramid

Classic Period: 300–900 A.D.

300–625 A.D.   They continue farming and building cities.
They build their first **pyramids**.

625–800 A.D.   They develop
- writing methods
- sculpture
- pottery
- **architecture**
- accurate calendars

Maya civilization reaches its peak.

800–900 A.D.   They leave cities and move to farmland.
Classic Mayan civilization collapses.

Postclassic Period: 900–1530 A.D.

900–950 A.D.	The Maya nearly die out. Reasons are unknown.
1190–1450 A.D.	The Maya continue to grow on the Yucatán.
1460 A.D.	A major hurricane hits the Yucatán. Crops and buildings are destroyed.
1470 A.D.	A **plague** hits. Many lives are lost.
1519 A.D.	The Spanish conquest begins.
1520 A.D.– *Present*	**Descendants** of the ancient Maya live in Mexico.

Mother and daughter in the marketplace

Chapter 2

Ancient City Life

City of Tikal, Guatemala

Cities

During the Classic Period, about 40 Mayan cities could be found. Between 5,000 and 60,000 people lived in each city.

11

Tikal pyramid, Guatemala

Tikal was one of the largest. It covered an area of six square miles. It contained about 10,000 structures. These were everything from small huts to grand pyramids.

How Did Tikal Compare?

Tikal had about 60,000 citizens. Its **population density** was several times greater than an average city in America or Europe at the same time.

Mayan cities were unplanned. They simply grew as needed.

The Maya tore down and rebuilt structures to keep up with cities' changing needs.

They rarely built walls around cities. But they did connect major sites with stone roads.

The Buildings

All cities had these features.

- shrines
- ball courts
- pyramids
- plazas
- temples
- palaces
- homes
- markets

Ball court, Chichén Itzá

Mayan pyramids

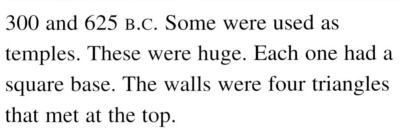

Pyramids

The Maya started building pyramids sometime between 300 and 625 B.C. Some were used as temples. These were huge. Each one had a square base. The walls were four triangles that met at the top.

Building a pyramid was no easy task. The Maya did everything by hand. People carried every single stone. There were no wheeled vehicles or cranes. The Maya didn't even use animals to help carry heavy loads.

There were several small rooms in each pyramid. Each pyramid had a deck near the top. People watched the stars from there.

Some pyramids told the story of the ruling family. The story was carved in hieroglyphics on a wall or into the stairs.

The Pyramid of the Magician in Northern Yucatán is made of five structures. Each was built on top of another. This may have taken 300 years to build!

Homes

The Maya built solid structures from stone. Their tools were also made of stone.

Politicians, warriors, and **nobility** lived in large palaces. The outsides were beautiful. They were painted red, white, yellow, and green. Some featured detailed carvings of fruit, **serpents**, and animals.

Serpent face

15

False columns surrounded some palaces. Most palaces had one or two **courtyards**.

Palace insides were usually simple. The dozens of rooms were small and damp. They had few windows. Air and light came in through doorways.

Walls were painted with **murals** or **graffiti**. Or they were covered in plain **stucco**.

Typical Maya lived in small one-room homes. These were made of reeds and stucco. They had **thatched** roofs. Such homes survived frequent earthquakes.

Thatched roof home

The Central Market

Each village or city had a central market. There people bought food, clothing, and items for the home. They paid for their goods with **cacao beans**.

You might have found these things for sale.

- animal skins
- feathers
- baskets
- medicines
- jewelry
- cushions
- masks
- rugs
- blankets
- meat
- tobacco
- pottery
- beeswax candles

Children on their way to the market

17

Thievery at the Market

Every culture has thieves. The Maya did too.

Crooks figured out how to cheat with the money. They filled cacao bean skins with clay. They kept the beans' "meat" for themselves. Then they offered the **counterfeit** beans as payment for goods.

Merchants accepted the clay beans. After all, they looked like the real thing.

They'd find out their mistake when they tried to make a chocolate drink from the beans. It didn't work, of course!

The People

Adults

Ancient Mayan citizens included

- rulers and other nobility
- priests
- warriors
- **scribes**
- artists
- public officials
- **merchants**
- farmers

The Maya adored their children. Birth was considered the most important Mayan event.

A baby was good luck to the Maya. He or she was also a sign of wealth. The more children you had, the more good luck—and wealth—you had.

Children

Little is known about the life of Mayan children. Boys and girls did many chores.

Girls helped their mothers in the home. They cooked and wove. Boys helped their fathers hunt and farm.

Kids probably made up their own games. Some children kept spider monkeys as pets.

A son helping his father plant corn

Sporting Events

The Maya built ball courts for their favorite sport, Pok-ol-pok. Adult men played this violent ball game.

Players wore padding. They hit a hard rubber ball between teams.

They were not allowed to use their hands. They could use their legs, hips, heads, arms, and shoulders.

The goal was to keep the ball in the air. The players also tried to hit the ball through a stone ring near the top of the court.

Ball court at Copan

At some point, the ball dropped to the ground. The team who missed it lost.

At best, men on the losing team lost their jewelry or clothes. At worst, the entire losing team was killed!

As you can see, the game was taken seriously. It drew huge, cheering crowds.

Onlookers bet on the game's outcome. People were known to bet their homes, their children, and themselves. They'd become **slaves** if they lost the bet!

Food

The Maya enjoyed a varied diet. They ate corn, beans, squash, and cacao. They baked bread and made tortillas. Other foods included

- chili peppers
- pumpkins
- beans
- tomatoes
- avocados
- papaya
- deer
- turkey

Clothing

Mayan men wore simple cloths. They draped them around their waists or over their entire bodies. Women wore dresses, or *huipil.*

For religious ceremonies, men "dressed up." They wore capes, jade jewelry, and headdresses.

Chapter 3

Trading Practices

Around 300 B.C., the Maya began exchanging goods, or *trading*, with others. They continued this practice until their decline.

The main trade route ran from the Gulf of

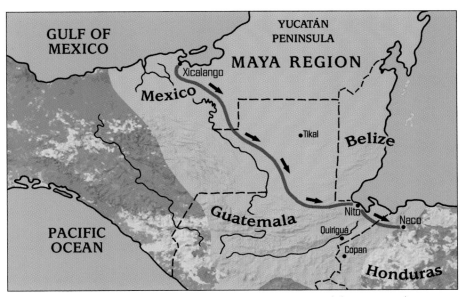

Mayan trade route

Mexico to Honduras.

Merchants traded many goods. Some were common. Some were rare and expensive. They included

- dried chili peppers
- salt
- honey
- animal skins, or *pelts*
- **manta**
- vegetable dyes
- **copal incense**

- herbal medicines
- **ceramics**
- feathers
- gold
- jade
- amber
- quartz

Jade

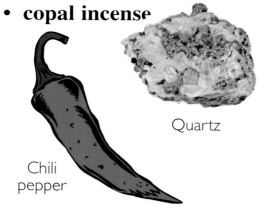
Quartz

Chili pepper

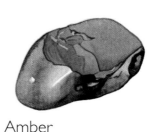
Amber

Merchants used money, or *legal tender*, while trading. Mayan legal tender included jade, cacao, and feathers sprinkled with gold dust.

24

Coastline at
Tulum

Trading by Water

The Maya took to the waters to trade.
How did they make their way?

They avoided the open ocean. They were
not sure that they could find their way back
if they lost sight of shore.

They traveled from bay to bay. This helped them mark their progress.

They sailed only in daylight. Each part of their trips lasted no longer than one day.

They developed signaling systems. They made bonfires on the beach. And they built lighthouses high in the trees.

Juan de Grijalva

Spanish **conquistador** Juan de Grijalva wrote, "We saw many clouds of smoke, one after another, laid out like signals. Then, farther on, we came to a town."

After the conquest, Bishop Diego de Landa wrote, "The Indians put signals in the trees to point out the way for boats sailing between Tabasco and Yucatán."

We know that the Maya drew maps. The Spanish found and wrote about them. Sadly, the Spanish also destroyed them.

A Spaniard once reported that a Mayan trade route map marked these spots.

- trade centers
- stops between trade centers
- villages
- towns
- cities
- shrines

Weather Report

It is amazing that the Maya were so successful at water travel. They were brave to even try it. Especially since the weather could really make it dangerous.

The Mayan area was often hit with **hurricanes** and other tropical storms. These happened anytime between summer and early winter.

In December and January, the weather turned colder. The area experienced the *nortes*. This is a type of winter storm. It is caused by cold air moving in from the north. Wind speeds can reach up to 50 miles per hour.

Chapter 4

Mythology, Religion, and—Corn?

The Maya had strong religious beliefs. And they created their own **mythology**. The myths helped explain and guide their lives.

They had many gods. All were respected and admired. Some were feared. Here are a few of them.

- Ah Kin was the Sun God. He watched over the day.

- Chac was the Rain God.

- Ix Chel was the Moon Goddess. She helped women weave. She also protected children.

- Kukulcan was the Founding God. He created civilization.

- The Jaguar God ruled the Underworld, or home of the dead. He could turn into the Sun God.

Chac (long-nosed Rain God) on Nunnery, Uxmal

The Power of the Jaguar God

The Maya believed that the Jaguar God was powerful.

According to mythology, he turned himself into the Sun God each day.

Early in the morning, he began traveling across the sky. He went as far west as he could. Then he disappeared. And it was dark.

This explained the rising and setting of the sun. The Maya believed that the Sun God turned back into the Jaguar God at nightfall. Then the Jaguar God fell back into the Underworld.

With each new day, the process repeated.

Jaguar temple, Tikal

Maya worshipped gods in their temples.
They also used the temples to make
predictions about the stars.

They prayed. They made offerings to their gods daily. They **sacrificed** food, jewels, animals—and sometimes humans. They also performed ritual bloodlettings and torture.

All this was an attempt to keep the gods happy. The Maya believed that doing so would keep the world safe from **chaos**.

Modern Maya can be found in Mexico, Guatemala, Belize, Honduras, and El Salvador.

Many Maya of today still follow some of the ancient practices.

How Does Corn Fit In?

Corn was more than just a big part of the Mayan diet. It was also an important religious symbol.

Growing corn was considered a sacred duty. Those who raised it felt honored. Why? Because corn was a gift from the gods.

The sacred book of the Maya is called *Popol Vuh*. It says that humankind itself was made of corn.

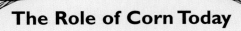

The Role of Corn Today

Corn is still the most basic piece of the Mayan diet. About 50 to 70 percent of Mayan food is corn-based. In fact, more than 400 common Mayan recipes use corn!

People also add corn to homemade **salves** and **tonics**. They use these to treat **warts**, tumors, kidney problems, **hepatitis**, and **diabetes**.

The "Slash and Burn" Method

The Maya of long ago used the "slash and burn" agricultural method with corn crops.

- The Maya selected a plot.

- They removed low vegetation with a small ax, or *machete*.

- They cut down large trees. They left cottonwoods, though. These trees were sacred. They also left a few fruit trees.

33

The steps on page 33 are the "slash" part of the method. Next comes the "burn."

They burned the dead vegetation once it dried. The field was clear and ready to be planted. The ash provided needed "food" for the soil.

The Maya had to trust their calendar of the seasons. The planting method had to take place at just the right time. The "right time" was in the dry season *just before* the rains came.

If they made a mistake, the Maya risked losing their crops.

Corn in Mythology

This myth explains how corn came to the Maya.

Corn was hidden under a huge rock. Humans could not see it.

One day, a rat followed a trail of ants to the rock. The ants were eating corn. They told the rat that corn was good food.

The rat could not move the rock. Neither could his friend the woodpecker. The woodpecker was injured while trying. His head was caught under the rock for a bit. (That's how he came to have a red head. The bloodstain has been there ever since.)

The rat decided to tell the humans about the corn. He thought they might be strong enough to move the rock.

The humans tried. But they could not move the rock either. It was too big and too heavy. They asked for the gods' help. Chac, the Rain God, was able to help. Then he and other gods presented corn to humans as a gift.

Soon, a God of Corn entered Mayan mythology. His name was Yum K'aax. He was a young man. His hair was long and silky. He wore a headdress. It was made of a cornstalk surrounded by leaves.

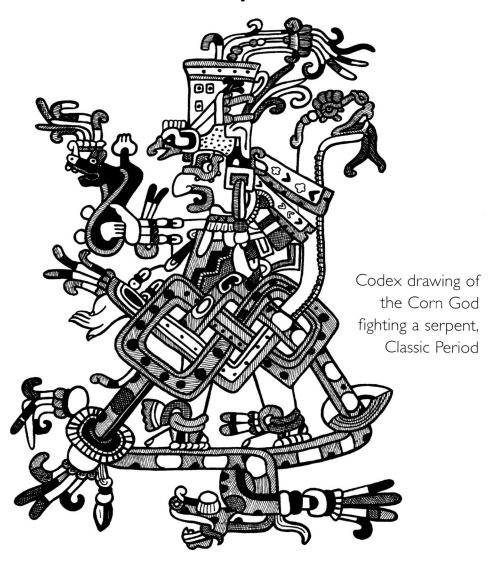

Codex drawing of the Corn God fighting a serpent, Classic Period

Chapter 5

Arts and Sciences

Spoken Language

There were about 40 known Mayan languages. Yucatec is one of the most important. It is still spoken in some parts of the Yucatán.

Letter Sounds

Mayan Letter	Sounds Like
a	*o* as in "m*o*p"
e	*e* as in "p*e*t"
i	*ee* as in "s*ee*n"
o	*o* as in "g*o*"
oo	*o*; same sound as the letter *o* but held longer
u	*oo* as in "m*oo*n"
x	*sh* as in "a*sh*"

Everyday Sayings

In Mayan	In English
Bix a belex?	Hi, how are you?
Maloob.	I am fine.
Yum botic.	Thank you.
Mixba.	You are welcome.
Tu'x ka binex?	Where are you going?
Kin bin tin nah.	I am going home.
Koox tun.	Let's get going.

Writing System and Books

The Maya used an advanced writing system of hieroglyphics. These are also known as glyphs. Glyphs are picturelike symbols that stand for words and ideas.

Maya carved and painted glyphs on pyramids, temples, and pottery. They recorded dates and significant events in rulers' lives.

Glyphs were used from the 3rd to the 17th century A.D. There were 800 signs. **Scholars** can read about two-thirds of Mayan writing.

A Mayan book is a *codex*. A codex was likely to contain writing about

- gods
- history
- daily life
- religious ceremonies
- medicine
- **astronomy**

The plural form of *codex* is *codices*. Only four Mayan codices have survived. The Spanish destroyed the rest in the 16th century.

Detail from a codex

The Four Surviving Codices

The codices are written in glyphs. They are made of fig-bark paper and folded like an accordion. Covers are made of jaguar skin.

The books deal with astronomy and ritual. Surviving books include

- *Dresden Codex.* This was probably written in the 11th or 12th century A.D. It is a copy of earlier 5th- to 9th-century texts.
- *Madrid Codex.* This was written in the 15th century.
- *Paris Codex.* This is slightly older than the *Madrid Codex.*
- *Grolier Codex.* This was not discovered until 1971. It was written in the 13th century.

Ceramics and Pottery

In the Classic Period, ceramic artists were educated. People respected the artists' work. They were also willing to pay for it.

Artists created the pottery. Then they painted on scenes from myths, mathematics, and religion. Paint was made from ground **pigment**, clay, and water.

Mayan citizens used clay pots for cooking and storing food. They used ceramics as

- decoration
- tableware
- offerings to the dead
- legal tender
- symbols of wealth

Mayan pottery

Astronomy and the Calendar

The Maya were skilled astronomers. They plotted the stars. And they figured out the positions of the moon and Venus.

Their calendars were accurate. They had both religious and solar calendars. These were used for rituals and daily life.

Mathematics

The Maya had two systems of symbols for numbers. The most commonly used system was made up of bars and dots. A bar had a value of five. A dot had a value of one.

The numbers from 1 to 19 looked like this.

The Maya used addition, subtraction, multiplication, and division. They used whole numbers up to about 1 billion.

They also used the principle of the number zero. Only two other peoples in history used this principle. They were the Hindus and the Babylonians.

The use of zero spread throughout the world from these three cultures.

Chapter 6

The Spanish Conquest

The Spanish invaded the Yucatán Peninsula in the 16th century A.D. *Conquistadores* stormed in. These soldiers were to move through—and conquer—the Americas.

The great Maya civilization had declined around the year 900. That was more than 600 years before the conquistadores arrived. Since that time, the Maya had suffered greatly. They'd lost people to disease, **famine**, and natural disaster.

The conquistadores found it easy to move in. The Maya still practiced their religion, spoke their **traditional** language, and recorded their history in glyphs.

Here is how the Spanish invaded the area.

- Hernán Cortés led 500 men and 16 horses into Mexico's Aztec empire. They arrived in 1519. They finally conquered the Aztec in 1522.
- Pedro de Alvarado invaded Guatemala.
- Francisco Pizarro had 180 men and 37 horses. He defeated the Incas in Peru in 1531.
- Diego de Almagro invaded Chile in 1536.

At this point, Spanish rule spread over much of Central and South America.

The conquistadores happily wrecked many native civilizations. They did the same to the Maya. They tore down buildings and built over ruins.

As mentioned earlier, the Spanish destroyed Mayan writings.

How did that happen? A Spanish bishop named Diego de Landa tried to force the Maya to give up their beliefs. They refused. So he burned all of their books.

Franciscan convent in Mani, where Bishop Diego de Landa burned the Mayan codices

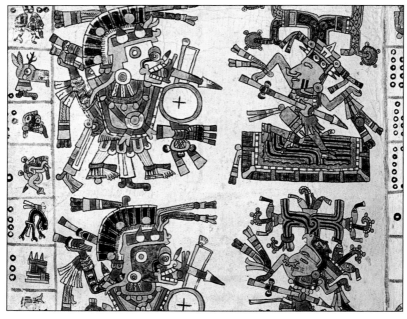

Detail from a codex

This is the main reason that we have so little information about the Maya.

Luckily, the Maya saved a few books. They had to sneak them away from the Spanish. They hid the codices in caves.

Somehow, the books ended up in Europe. This was no doubt the doing of proud Maya trying to save what was left of their history.

Over the years, the books have decayed. The pictures are now completely gone. But their words help tell the splendid story of the mysterious Maya.

That's one story the world wants to know.

Just for Fun
The Dance of the Reeds

Try this Mayan game with a large group of friends. You could even perform it for an audience!

What You Will Need

You will need one person to be the judge, or *holpop*. The holpop should wear a colorful headdress and cloak.

You will need 10 to 20 dancers. Each dancer needs a bundle of "reeds." (Make them yourself. Be creative!)

You will also need several musicians. Each one needs an instrument. We don't know exactly which instruments the Maya had. But below are ones that should be easy to find today.

- wooden drum
- rattle
- tambourine
- maracas
- bell
- triangle

How to Play

1. The dancers form a circle. Each one puts his or her right hand on the next dancer's shoulder. Each dancer holds a bundle of reeds in his or her left hand.

2. When the music starts, the dancers move to the right. They move to the beat of the music. They stay in the circle. They also wave their reeds.

3. The holpop walks around the outside of the circle. He or she taps one dancer on the shoulder. That dancer is the "hunter."

4. Next, the holpop taps the "hunted" on the shoulder.

5. The "hunter" and "hunted" move to the inside of the circle. They continue moving to the music. They wave their reeds.

6. The holpop claps. (He or she chooses when to do it.) The music stops. The dancers stop, face in, and wave their reeds at the "hunter" and "hunted."

7. The "hunter" tries to tag the "hunted" with the reeds.

8. Once tagged, the "hunted" becomes the "hunter." The other dancer returns to the circle.

9. The holpop taps another "hunted."

10. The game continues.

Maya Mystery Quiz: Which well-known game does this remind you of?

Answer: Duck-Duck-Goose

Glossary

agriculture   practice of growing crops and raising livestock

archaeologist   one who studies past civilizations

architecture   art and science of building

artifact   something created by humans for practical use

astronomy   study of the solar system

cacao beans   dried seeds of a South American evergreen used for making cocoa and chocolate

ceramics   items, such as pottery and dishes, that are made from clay and baked at a high temperature

chaos   state of confusion

conquistador   Spanish soldier in the conquest of the Americas in the 16th century A.D.

copal incense   part of a tree burned for its aroma

counterfeit   fake or imitation

courtyard   enclosed space next to a building

culture   group's set of shared attitudes, values, and practices

descendant   one who is related through past generations

diabetes   disease that causes high levels of sugar in the blood

educated guess   opinion based on related knowledge about the topic

famine	extreme shortage of food
graffiti	messages or drawings, usually made on public surfaces
hepatitis	disease of the liver
hieroglyphics	writing system that uses pictures for words
hurricane	storm in the western Atlantic ocean; winds reach 74 miles per hour or more
manta	square cloth used as a shawl
merchant	one who sells goods
mural	large artwork, such as a painting, that is applied directly to a wall or ceiling
mythology	body of traditional (see glossary entry) stories
nobility	group of people given higher status than others

peninsula	portion of land sticking out into the water
pigment	material that gives color
plague	contagious disease that results in a great number of deaths
population density	number of people living in an area of a specific, measured size
pyramid	structure with a square base and four triangular walls that meet at the top
ruins	remains of something destroyed
sacrifice	to offer as a gift

salve	ointment
scholar	one who has knowledge
scribe	writer
serpent	snake
slave	someone forced to work for another person who "owns" him or her
stucco	plaster used to form a hard covering for walls
technology	useful application of knowledge
thatched	made from grasses or straw
tonic	liquid medicine
traditional	relating to beliefs or behavior handed down from one generation to another
wart	bump on the skin caused by a virus

Index